SPECTRUM SERIES
PHONICS

TABLE OF CONTENTS

SPECTRUM

Grand Rapids, Michigan

INSTRUCTIONAL CONSULTANT
Mary Lou Maples, Ed.D.
Chairman of Department of Education
Huntingdon College
Montgomery, Alabama

EDITORIAL AND PRODUCTION STAFF
Series Editor: Joyce R. Rhymer; *Project Editor:* Suzanne Senn Diehm; *Production Editor:*
Carole R. Hill; *Senior Designer:* Patrick J. McCarthy; *Associate Designer:* Terry D. Anderson;
Project Artist: Gilda Braxton Edwards; *Illustrators:* Lisy Boren, Ethel Gold

Frank Schaffer Publications®

Spectrum is an imprint of Frank Schaffer Publications.

Send all inquiries to: Frank Schaffer Publications • 3195 Wilson Drive NW • Grand Rapids, MI 49534

ISBN 1-56189-940-2   8 9 10 11 12 13 VHG 10 09 08 07 06

Organized for successful learning!

The SPECTRUM PHONICS SERIES builds the right skills for reading.

The program combines four important skill strands — phonics, structural analysis, vocabulary, and dictionary skills — so your students build the skills they need to become better readers.

Four types of lesson pages offer thorough, clearly focused, systematic skills practice. That means you can focus on just the skills that need work — for the whole class, a small group, or for individualized instruction.

The SPECTRUM PHONICS SERIES is easy for students to use independently.

Although phonics may be an important part of a reading program, sometimes there just isn't enough time to do it all. That's why PHONICS offers uncomplicated lessons your children can succeed with on their own.

Colorful borders capture interest, highlight essential information, and help organize lesson structure. And your children get off to a good start with concise explanations and clear directions . . . followed by sample answers that show them exactly what to do.

In addition, vocabulary has been carefully controlled so your children work with familiar words. Key pictures and key words are used consistently throughout the series to represent specific sounds. And a sound-symbol chart at the back of the text helps your students quickly recall sound-symbol relationships.

INSTRUCTION PAGE . . . The skill being covered is noted at the bottom of each student page for easy reference.

REINFORCEMENT PAGE . . .
Comprehension exercises that use context as well as phonics skills to help build the connection from decoding to comprehension.

Turn page for more information.

Easy to manage

REVIEW PAGES . . . Frequent reviews emphasize skills application.

ASSESSMENT PAGES . . . Assessment pages give you helpful feedback   on how your students are doing.

ANSWER KEY . . . Gives you the help you need when you need it — including student pages with answers for quick, easy reference.

Completing Pictures

Name_____

Directions: Complete each picture by tracing the dotted lines. Color each picture.

Eye-hand coordination

3

Moving from Left to Right

Name_____

Directions: Beginning at the black dot, trace the dotted line in each picture, moving from left to right.

Left-to-right progression

Matching Pictures

Name_____

Directions: In each row, circle the picture that is the same as the first picture in the row.

Matching Pictures

Name _____

Directions: In each row, circle the picture that is the same as the first picture in the row.

6

Visual discrimination of pictures

Matching Letters

Name _____

| A a |  ant | B b | ball |

A V (A) H A

a a o a e

B B K T B

b f g b b

Directions: In each row, circle the letters that are the same as the first letter in the row.

Matching Letters

Name_____

| A a | ant | B b | ball |

A	h	a	x	a
a	A	P	D	A
B	t	b	f	b
b	B	L	M	B

Directions: Look at the letter at the beginning of each row. Circle the letters in that row that belong with the first letter.

8

Matching capital with lowercase a and b

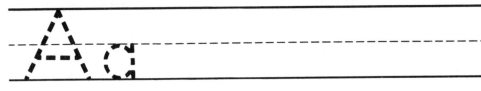

ant

Directions: Name the pictures. Circle each picture whose name begins with the sound you hear at the beginning of *ant*.

Auditory discrimination of initial short *a*

9

Short A

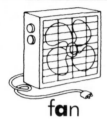
fan

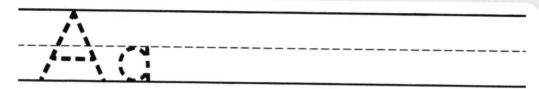

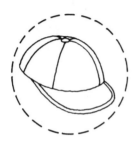   

 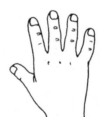  

Directions: Name the pictures. Circle each picture whose name has the sound you hear in the middle of *fan*.

10

Auditory discrimination of medial short *a*

Consonants: B

Name _____

 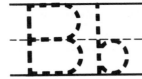

ball

Directions: Name the pictures. Circle each picture whose name begins with the sound you hear at the beginning of *ball.*

Auditory discrimination of initial *b*

11

Consonants: B

Name

B b

ball

b

Directions: Name the pictures. Write the letter *b* below each picture whose name begins with *b*.

12

Matching Letters

Name ______________________

Cc 
car

Dd 
dog

C	C	G	C	O
c	o	c	n	c
D	O	D	D	B
d	d	h	g	d

Directions: In each row, circle the letters that are the same as the first letter in the row.

Matching Letters

Name _____

C c	car	D d	dog

C	h	c	n	c

c	C	D	V	C

D	d	t	k	d

d	U	D	L	D

Directions: Look at the letter at the beginning of each row. Circle the letters in that row that belong with the first letter.

14

Matching capital with lowercase c and d

Consonants: C

Name _____

 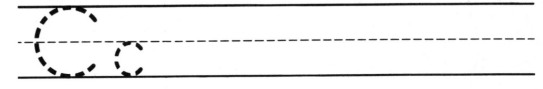

car

 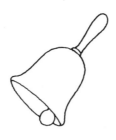  

Directions: Name the pictures. Circle each picture whose name begins with the sound you hear at the beginning of *car.*

Auditory discrimination of initial c

15

Consonants: *C*

Name _____

car

Directions: Name the pictures. Write the letter *c* below each picture whose name begins with *c*.

16

Sound-symbol association of initial *c*

Consonants: D

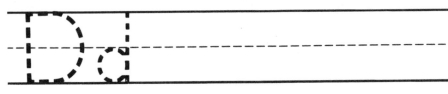

Name _____

dog

   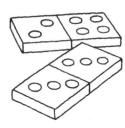

Directions: Name the pictures. Circle each picture whose name begins with the sound you hear at the beginning of *dog.*

Auditory discrimination of initial *d*

17

Consonants: D

Name _____

dog

Dd

d

Directions: Name the pictures. Write the letter *d* below each picture whose name begins with *d*.

Sound-symbol association of initial *d*

Matching Letters

Name _____

| E e
 elephant | F f
 fish |

E	(E)	F	B	E
e	a	e	v	e
F	T	E	F	F
f	f	l	f	k

Directions: In each row, circle the letters that are the same as the first letter in the row.

Visual discrimination of capital and lowercase *e* and *f*

19

Matching Letters

Name _____

E e **e**lephant	F f **f**ish

E	(e) n e o
e	M E H E
F	f h l f
f	A F T F

Directions: Look at the letter at the beginning of each row. Circle the letters in that row that belong with the first letter.

20

Matching capital with lowercase *e* and *f*

Short *E*

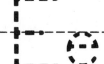

elephant

   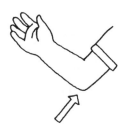

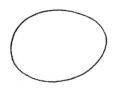   

Directions: Name the pictures. Circle each picture whose name begins with the sound you hear at the beginning of *elephant*.

Auditory discrimination of initial short *e*

Short *E*

bed

Directions: Name the pictures. Circle each picture whose name has the sound you hear in the middle of *bed*.

Auditory discrimination of medial short *e*

A and E

Name

Directions: Look at the picture at the beginning of each row. Circle each picture in the row whose name begins with the same sound as the first picture.

 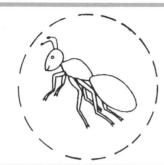  

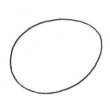   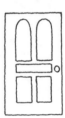

Directions: Look at the picture at the beginning of each row. Circle each picture in the row whose name has the same middle sound as the first picture.

  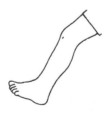 

Consonants: F

Name _____

 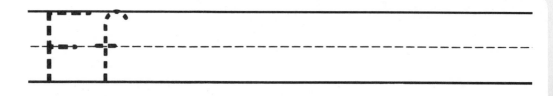

fish

   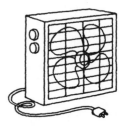

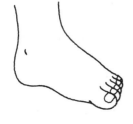  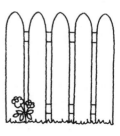

   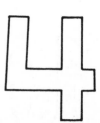

Directions: Name the pictures. Circle each picture whose name begins with the sound you hear at the beginning of *fish.*

24

Consonants: F

Name _____

fish

5

4

Directions: Name the pictures. Write the letter *f* below each picture whose name begins with *f*.

Sound-symbol association of initial *f*

25

B, C, D, F

Name _____

b			
c			
d			
f			

Directions: Look at the letter at the beginning of each row. Circle each picture in the row whose name begins with the sound made by that letter.

Review of sound-symbol association of initial *b, c, d,* and *f*

Matching Letters

Name _____

G g   goat   H h   horse

| G | C | G | F | G |

| g | g | y | g | j |

| H | H | L | I | H |

| h | d | h | h | l |

Directions: In each row, circle the letters that are the same as the first letter in the row.

Visual discrimination of capital and lowercase *g* and *h*

27

Matching Letters

Name _____

G g	H h

goat

horse

G	(g) d g y
g	Q G S G
H	k l h h
h	H A X H

Directions: Look at the letter at the beginning of each row. Circle the letters in that row that belong with the first letter.

28

Matching capital with lowercase *g* and *h*

Consonants: G

goat

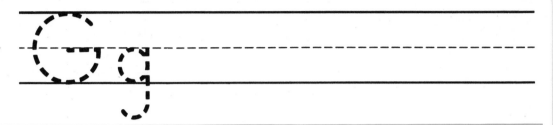

   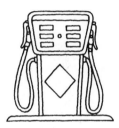

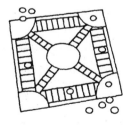   

Directions: Name the pictures. Circle each picture whose name begins with the sound you hear at the beginning of *goat*.

Auditory discrimination of initial *g*

29

Consonants: G

Name

goat

G g

g

Directions: Name the pictures. Write the letter *g* below each picture whose name begins with *g*.

Sound-symbol association of initial *g*

Consonants: H

Name _____

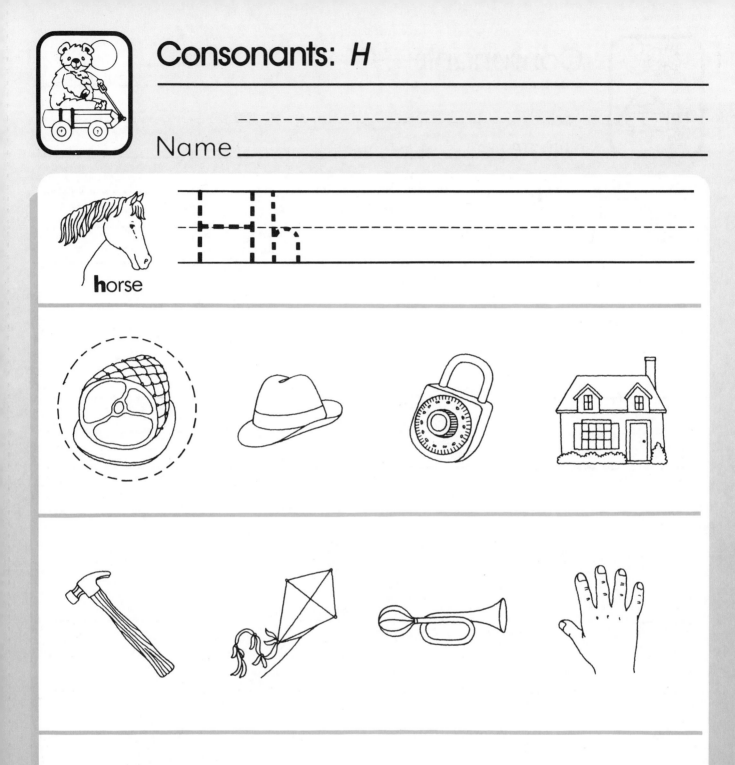

horse

Directions: Name the pictures. Circle each picture whose name begins with the sound you hear at the beginning of *horse*.

Auditory discrimination of initial *h*

31

Consonants: H

Name _____

horse

Directions: Name the pictures. Write the letter *h* below each picture whose name begins with *h*.

Sound-symbol association of initial *h*

Matching Letters

Name _____

I i
igloo

J j
jet

| I | (I) | H | T | I |

| i | i | r | i | t |

| J | U | J | L | J |

| j | j | p | j | q |

Directions: In each row, circle the letters that are the same as the first letter in the row.

I i	igloo	J j	jet
I	t	(i)	i r
i	I	V H I	
J	i j	p j	
j	U	J J L	

Directions: Look at the letter at the beginning of each row. Circle the letters in that row that belong with the first letter.

Matching capital with lowercase *i* and *j*

Short *I*

Name _____

 I i

 **i**gloo

 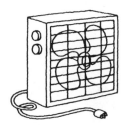 

Directions: Name the pictures. Circle each picture whose name begins with the sound you hear at the beginning of *igloo.*

Auditory discrimination of initial short *i*

Short *I*

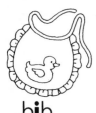

I i

bib

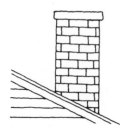

Directions: Name the pictures. Circle each picture whose name has the sound you hear in the middle of *bib*.

Auditory discrimination of medial short *i*

Consonants: *J*

Name _____

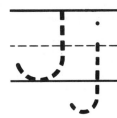

jet

  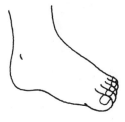

 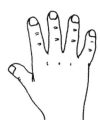  

Directions: Name the pictures. Circle each picture whose name begins with the sound you hear at the beginning of *jet*.

Auditory discrimination of initial *j*

Consonants: *J*

Name _____

jet

J j

j

Directions: Name the pictures. Write the letter *j* below each picture whose name begins with *j*.

Sound-symbol association of initial *j*

Matching Letters

Name _____

K k  **k**itten   L l **l**ion

K	(K)	N	R	K
k	k	l	k	t
L	J	L	I	L
l	b	l	l	d

Directions: In each row, circle the letters that are the same as the first letter in the row.

Matching Letters

Name_____

| K k | **k**itten | L l | **l**ion |

K	$\big(\,k\,\big)$ h k f
k	H K Y K
L	l h f l
l	L T L J

Directions: Look at the letter at the beginning of each row. Circle the letters in that row that belong with the first letter.

40

Matching capital with lowercase k and l

Consonants: K

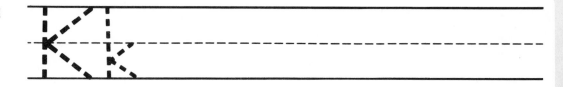

kitten

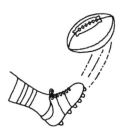

Directions: Name the pictures. Circle each picture whose name begins with the sound you hear at the beginning of *kitten.*

Auditory discrimination of initial *k*

41

Consonants: *K*

Name _____

kitten

Directions: Name the pictures. Write the letter *k* below each picture whose name begins with *k*.

Sound-symbol association of initial *k*

G, H, J, K

Name _____

g			
h			
j			
k			

Directions: Look at the letter at the beginning of each row. Circle each picture in the row whose name begins with the sound made by that letter.

Review of sound-symbol association of initial *g, h, j,* and *k*

Consonants: L

Name _____

 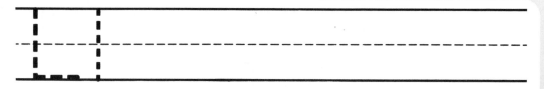

lion

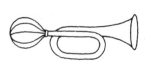   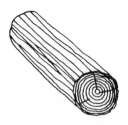

Directions: Name the pictures. Circle each picture whose name begins with the sound you hear at the beginning of *lion.*

44

Consonants: *L*

Name _____

l lion

Directions: Name the pictures. Write the letter *l* below each picture whose name begins with *l*.

Sound-symbol association of initial *l*

45

Matching Letters

Name _____

M	m	mouse	N	n	nest

M	W	(M)	H	M

m	m	h	w	m

N	V	N	N	M

n	n	m	u	n

Directions: In each row, circle the letters that are the same as the first letter in the row.

Visual discrimination of capital and lowercase *m* and *n*

Matching Letters

Name _____

M m	**N** n
mouse	nest

M	n m r m
m	M K M N
N	n m n h
n	Y N W N

Directions: Look at the letter at the beginning of each row. Circle the letters in that row that belong with the first letter.

Matching capital with lowercase *m* and *n*

47

mouse

 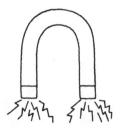  

Directions: Name the pictures. Circle each picture whose name begins with the sound you hear at the beginning of *mouse*.

Auditory discrimination of initial *m*

Consonants: *M*

Name _____

mouse

Mm _____

m _____

Directions: Name the pictures. Write the letter *m* below each picture whose name begins with *m*.

Sound-symbol association of initial *m*

49

Consonants: N

Name _____

nest

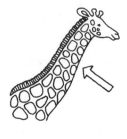   

Directions: Name the pictures. Circle each picture whose name begins with the sound you hear at the beginning of *nest.*

50   Auditory discrimination of initial *n*

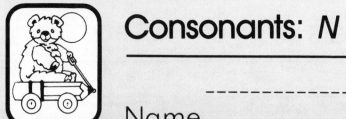

Consonants: N

Name _____

nest

Nn

n

Directions: Name the pictures. Write the letter *n* below each picture whose name begins with *n*.

Matching Letters

Name _____

O o
octopus

P p
pig

O	O	Q	C	O

o	c	o	u	o

P	B	P	P	R

p	p	q	p	j

Directions: In each row, circle the letters that are the same as the first letter in the row.

Visual discrimination of capital and lowercase *o* and *p*

Matching Letters

Name _____

O o

octopus

P p

pig

O	(o)	p	o	c
o	Q	O	U	O
P	p	y	o	p
p	D	P	P	B

Directions: Look at the letter at the beginning of each row. Circle the letters in that row that belong with the first letter.

Matching capital with lowercase *o* and *p*

53

Short O

octopus

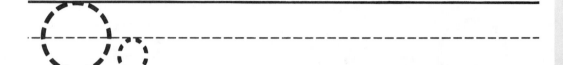

5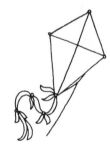

Directions: Name the pictures. Circle each picture whose name begins with the sound you hear at the beginning of *octopus.*

54

Auditory discrimination of initial short *o*

Short O

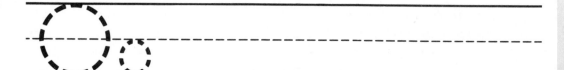

Name _____

top

 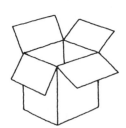  

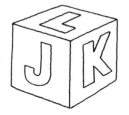   

Directions: Name the pictures. Circle each picture whose name has the sound you hear in the middle of *top.*

Auditory discrimination of medial short *o*

55

I and O

Name _____

Directions: Look at the picture at the beginning of each row. Circle each picture in the row whose name begins with the same sound as the first picture.

Directions: Look at the picture at the beginning of each row. Circle each picture in the row whose name has the same middle sound as the first picture.

 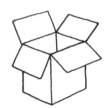  

Review of auditory discrimination of short *i* and short *o* in initial and medial positions

Consonants: *P*

Name _____

P p

pig

Directions: Name the pictures. Circle each picture whose name begins with the sound you hear at the beginning of *pig.*

Auditory discrimination of initial *p*

57

Name _____

P p

pig

P

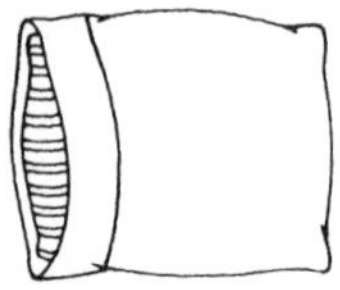

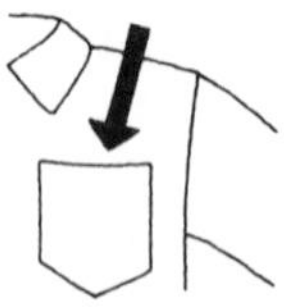

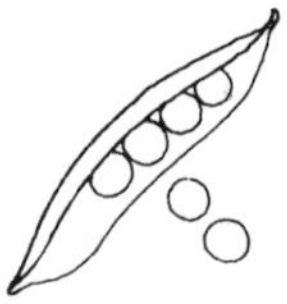

Directions: Name the pictures. Write the letter *p* below each picture whose name begins with *p*.

Sound-symbol association of initial *p*

REVIEW

L, M, N, P

Name

l			
m			
n			
p			

Directions: Look at the letter at the beginning of each row. Circle each picture in the row whose name begins with the sound made by that letter.

Review of sound-symbol association of initial *l, m, n,* and *p*

59

Matching Letters

Name _____

Q q
quilt

R r
rose

Q	Q	O	D	Q
q	q	j	q	p
R	P	R	B	R
r	h	r	r	m

Directions: In each row, circle the letters that are the same as the first letter in the row.

Visual discrimination of capital and lowercase *q* and *r*

Matching Letters

Name _____

Q q		R r
quilt		**r**ose

Q	e	(q)	q	d

q	Q	O	U	Q

R	r	n	m	r

r	P	R	B	R

Directions: Look at the letter at the beginning of each row. Circle the letters in that row that belong with the first letter.

Matching capital with lowercase q and r

61

Consonants: *Qu*

Name _____

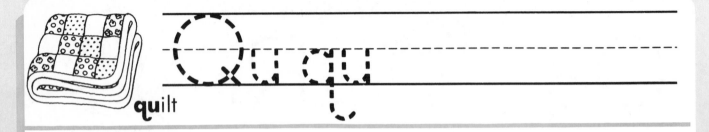

 **qu**ilt

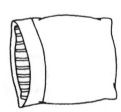

Directions: Name the pictures. Circle each picture whose name begins with the sound you hear at the beginning of *quilt.*

62

Auditory discrimination of initial *qu*

Consonants: *Qu*

Qu qu

quilt

Directions: Name the pictures. Write the letters *qu* below each picture whose name begins with *qu*.

Sound-symbol association of initial *qu*

63

Consonants: *R*

Name

 **r**ose

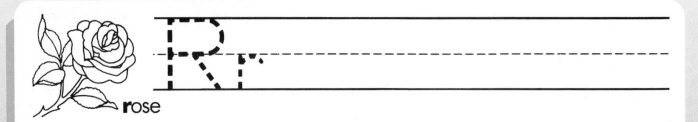

  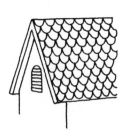 

Directions: Name the pictures. Circle each picture whose name begins with the sound you hear at the beginning of *rose.*

64

Auditory discrimination of initial *r*

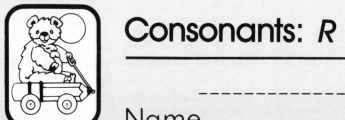

Consonants: R

Name_____

R r rose

r

Directions: Name the pictures. Write the letter *r* below each picture whose name begins with *r*.

Matching Letters

S s	☀ **s**un	T t	⛺ **t**ent
S	(S) Z G S
s	z s e s
T	T L T Y
t	h t t l

Directions: In each row, circle the letters that are the same as the first letter in the row.

Visual discrimination of capital and lowercase s and t

Matching Letters

| S s | ☼ **s**un | T t | ⛺ **t**ent |

| S | Ⓢ | c | s | o |

| s | G | S | C | S |

| T | l | t | t | i |

| t | T | Y | T | X |

Directions: Look at the letter at the beginning of each row. Circle the letters in that row that belong with the first letter.

Matching capital with lowercase *s* and *t*

Consonants: S

Name _____

sun

 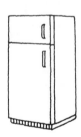 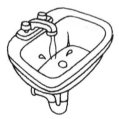 

Directions: Name the pictures. Circle each picture whose name begins with the sound you hear at the beginning of *sun.*

Auditory discrimination of initial *s*

Consonants: *S*

Name _____

sun

Ss

s

7

Directions: Name the pictures. Write the letter *s* below each picture whose name begins with *s*.

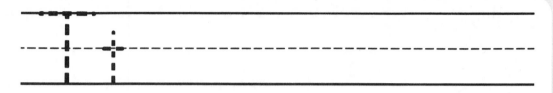

Name_____

tent

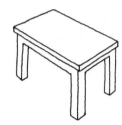

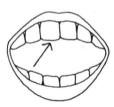

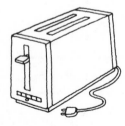

Directions: Name the pictures. Circle each picture whose name begins with the sound you hear at the beginning of *tent.*

70

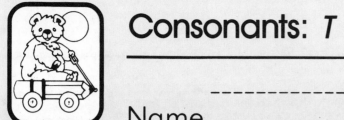

Consonants: *T*

Name _____

tent

Directions: Name the pictures. Write the letter *t* below each picture whose name begins with *t*.

Qu, R, S, T

Name

qu	
r	
s	
t	

Directions: Look at the letter or letters at the beginning of each row. Circle each picture in the row whose name begins with the sound made by that letter.

Review of sound-symbol association of initial *qu, r, s,* and *t*

Matching Letters

Name _____

| U u | umbrella | V v | vase |

U O (U) J U

u u n c u

V X V V N

v v u z v

Directions: In each row, circle the letters that are the same as the first letter in the row.

Visual discrimination of capital and lowercase *u* and *v*

Matching Letters

Name_____

U u		V v

umbrella

vase

U	v	u	n	u

u	U	O	U	C

V	w	v	u	v

v	V	N	Y	V

Directions: Look at the letter at the beginning of each row. Circle the letters in that row that belong with the first letter.

Matching capital with lowercase u and v

Short *U*

 **u**mbrella

 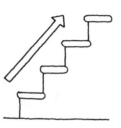  

  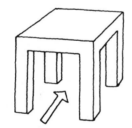 

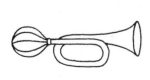   

Directions: Name the pictures. Circle each picture whose name begins with the sound you hear at the beginning of *umbrella.*

Auditory discrimination of initial short *u*

Name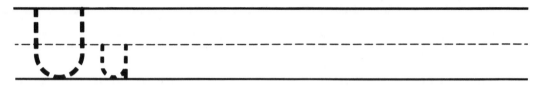

cup

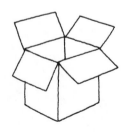   

Directions: Name the pictures. Circle each picture whose name has the sound you hear in the middle of *cup*.

Auditory discrimination of medial short *u*

REVIEW

Short *U*

Name _____

Directions: Look at the picture at the beginning of each row. Circle each picture in the row whose name begins with the same sound as the first picture.

 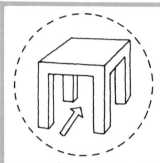  

Directions: Look at the picture at the beginning of each row. Circle each picture in the row whose name has the same middle sound as the first picture.

 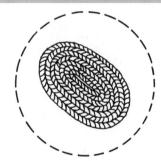  

Consonants: V

Name _____

vase

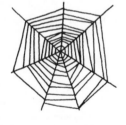

Directions: Name the pictures. Circle each picture whose name begins with the sound you hear at the beginning of *vase.*

Auditory discrimination of initial *v*

Name_____

vase

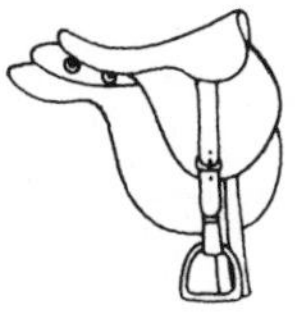

Directions: Name the pictures. Write the letter *v* below each picture whose name begins with *v*.

Matching Letters

Name_____

W w **watch**   X x **ax**

W	N	(W)	Y	W
w	w	v	x	w
X	Z	X	X	Y
x	x	y	x	t

Directions: In each row, circle the letters that are the same as the first letter in the row.

Visual discrimination of capital and lowercase *w* and *x*

Matching Letters

Name _____

W w	watch	X x	ax

| W | v | (w) | m | w |

| w | W | K | W | Z |

| X | x | t | v | x |

| x | Y | X | Z | X |

Directions: Look at the letter at the beginning of each row. Circle the letters in that row that belong with the first letter.

Matching capital with lowercase *w* and *x*

81

Consonants: W

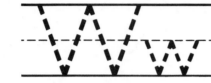

watch

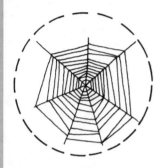   

   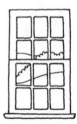

Directions: Name the pictures. Circle each picture whose name begins with the sound you hear at the beginning of *watch.*

82

Consonants: *W*

Name_____

watch

6

Directions: Name the pictures. Write the letter *w* below each picture whose name begins with *w*.

Sound-symbol association of initial *w*

83

Consonants: X

Name_____

a**x**

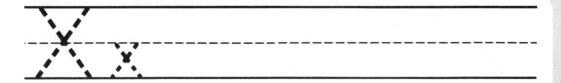

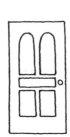

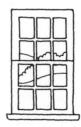

Directions: Name the pictures. Circle each picture whose name ends with the sound you hear at the end of *ax.*

Consonants: X

Name_____

a**x**

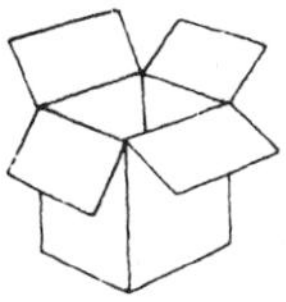

X X

_____

X

_____

_____

_____

_____

_____

_____

_____

_____

_____

_____

_____

_____

Directions: Name the pictures. Write the letter *x* below each picture whose name ends with *x*.

Matching Letters

Name _____

Y y

yard

Z z

zoo

Y	Ⓨ	T	K	Y

y	v	y	w	y

Z	Z	N	Z	I

z	z	s	w	z

Directions: In each row, circle the letters that are the same as the first letter in the row.

Visual discrimination of capital and lowercase *y* and *z*

Y y  **y**ard   Z z  **z**oo

Y	x	y	h	y
y	Y	T	Y	K
Z	s	z	z	c
z	N	Z	I	Z

Directions: Look at the letter at the beginning of each row. Circle the letters in that row that belong with the first letter.

Matching capital with lowercase y and z

Name_____

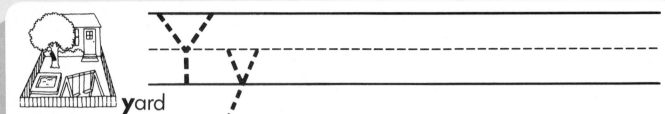

yard

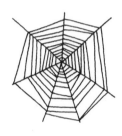  

Directions: Name the pictures. Circle each picture whose name begins with the sound you hear at the beginning of *yard.*

88

Auditory discrimination of initial *y*

Consonants: Y

Name _____

yard

y Y

6

Directions: Name the pictures. Write the letter *y* below each picture whose name begins with *y*.

Sound-symbol association of initial *y*

89

Consonants: Z

Name _____

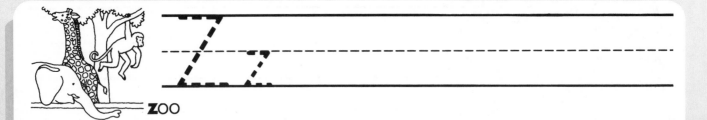

zoo

   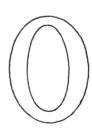

Directions: Name the pictures. Circle each picture whose name begins with the sound you hear at the beginning of *zoo.*

Auditory discrimination of initial *z*

Consonants: Z

Name

Zoo

Z

Directions: Name the pictures. Write the letter z below each picture whose name begins with z.

V, W, X, Y, Z

Name _____

V			
W			
X			
Y			
Z			

Directions: Look at the letter at the beginning of each row. Circle each picture in the row whose name has the sound made by that letter.

Review of sound-symbol association of initial *v*, *w*, final *x*, initial *y*, and *z*

Consonants

Name _____

(r) f v	b k x	b c t
h j n	g j z	r d t
m p v	n s w	j m n
d f g	qu r y ?	l v z

Directions: Name the pictures. Circle the letter that stands for the sound at the beginning of each picture name.

Assessment of sound-symbol association of initial consonants

Consonants

Name _____

k
p
v

t
y
z

c
d
f

d
s
v

b
n
h

j
l
s

d
t
w

c
g
l

f
r
z

l
n
y

b
k
w

x
j
m

Directions: Name the pictures. Circle the letter that stands for the sound at the beginning of each picture name.

Vowels

Name _____

Directions: Name the first picture in each row. Then circle all the pictures in that row that begin with the same sound as the first picture.

Assessment of auditory discrimination of initial vowels

95

Sounds and Letters

ant   **b**all   **c**ar   **d**og   **e**lephant

fish   **g**oat   **h**orse   **i**gloo   **j**et

kitten   **l**ion   **m**ouse   **n**est   **o**ctopus

pig   **qu**ilt   **r**ose   **s**un   **t**ent

umbrella   **v**ase   **w**atch   a**x**   **y**ard   **z**oo

Completing Pictures

Name

Directions: Complete each picture by tracing the dotted lines. Color each picture.

Eye-hand coordination   3

Moving from Left to Right

Name

Directions: Beginning at the black dot, trace the dotted line in each picture, moving from left to right.

4   Left-to-right progression

Matching Pictures

Name

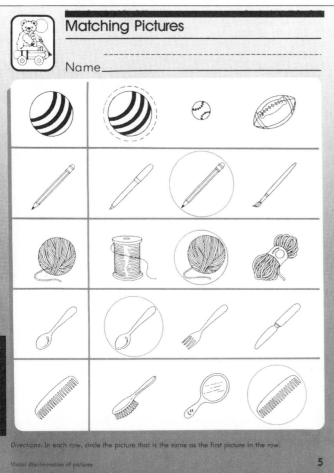

Directions: In each row, circle the picture that is the same as the first picture in the row.

Visual discrimination of pictures   5

Matching Pictures

Name

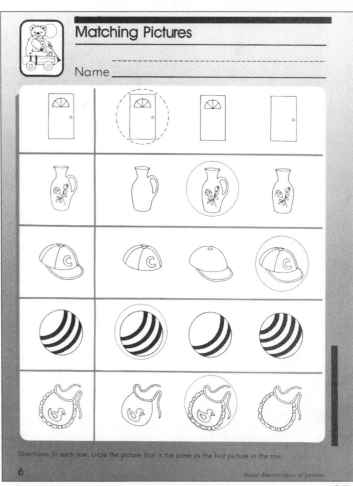

Directions: In each row, circle the picture that is the same as the first picture in the row.

6   Visual discrimination of pictures

Matching Letters

Name _____

Directions: In each row, circle the letters that are the same as the first letter in the row.

Visual discrimination of capital and lowercase *a* and *b*

7

Matching Letters

Name _____

Directions: Look at the letter at the beginning of each row. Circle the letters in that row that belong with the first letter.

8

Matching capital with lowercase *a* and *b*

Short A

Name _____

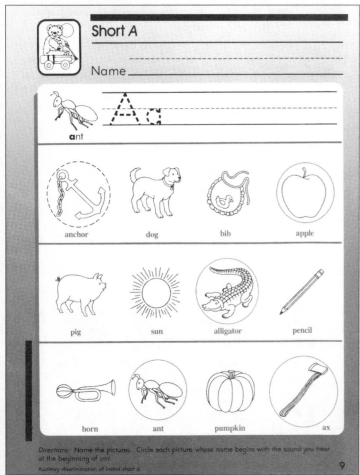

ant

anchor	dog	bib	apple
pig	sun	alligator	pencil
horn	ant	pumpkin	ax

Directions: Name the pictures. Circle each picture whose name begins with the sound you hear at the beginning of *ant*.

Auditory discrimination of initial short *a*.

9

Short A

Name _____

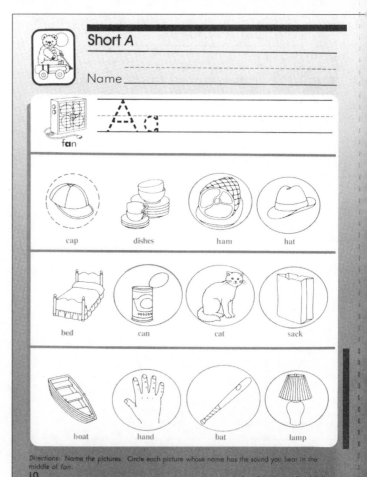

fan

cap	dishes	ham	hat
bed	can	cat	sack
boat	hand	bat	lamp

Directions: Name the pictures. Circle each picture whose name has the sound you hear in the middle of *fan*.

10

Auditory discrimination of medial short *a*

Name

B b

ball

balloon — cane — book — boy

bone — bird — mitten — bed

ax — bee — banana — belt

Directions: Name the pictures. Circle each picture whose name begins with the sound you hear at the beginning of *ball*.

Auditory discrimination of initial *b*

11

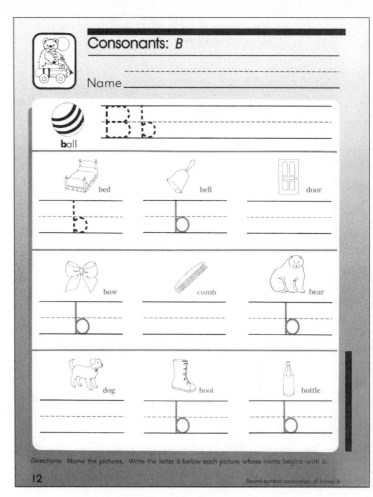

Name

B b

ball

bed — bell — door

bow — comb — bear

dog — boot — bottle

Directions: Name the pictures. Write the letter *b* below each picture whose name begins with *b*.

12

Sound-symbol association of initial *b*

Matching Letters

Name

C c car   **D d** dog

C | C G C O
c | o c n c
D | O D D B
d | d h g d

Directions: In each row, circle the letters that are the same as the first letter in the row.

Visual discrimination of capital and lowercase *c* and *d*

13

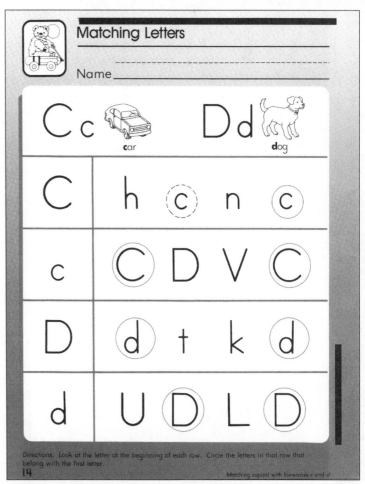

Matching Letters

Name

C c car   **D d** dog

C | h c n c
c | C D V C
D | d t k d
d | U D L D

Directions: Look at the letter at the beginning of each row. Circle the letters in that row that belong with the first letter.

14

Matching capital with lowercase *c* and *d*

99

Consonants: C

Name _____

car

Cc

coat   bell   cap   comb

candle   corn   pan   can

cow   cane   carrot   balloon

Directions: Name the pictures. Circle each picture whose name begins with the sound you hear at the beginning of *car*.
Auditory discrimination of initial *c*

15

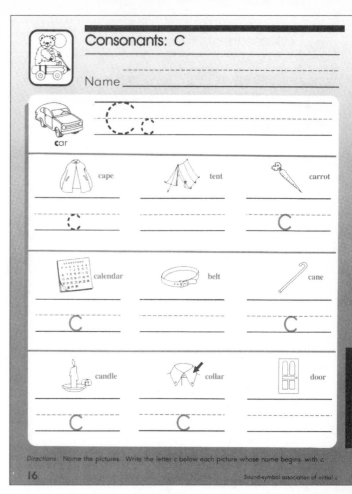

Consonants: C

Name _____

car

Cc

cape   tent   carrot

c   c

calendar   belt   cane

c   c

candle   collar   door

c   c

16

Directions: Name the pictures. Write the letter *c* below each picture whose name begins with *c*.
Sound-symbol association of initial *c*

Consonants: D

Name _____

dog

Dd

door   can   doll   dishes

balloon   desk   dive   dominoes

duck   dinosaur   pear   deer

Directions: Name the pictures. Circle each picture whose name begins with the sound you hear at the beginning of *dog*.
Auditory discrimination of initial *d*

17

Consonants: D

Name _____

dog

Dd

desk   doctor   four

d   d

dishes   comb   dinosaur

d   d

corn   door   deer

d   d

18

Directions: Name the pictures. Write the letter *d* below each picture whose name begins with *d*.
Sound-symbol association of initial *d*

Matching Letters

Name _____

E e elephant   F f fish

E	E	F	B	E
e	a	e	v	e
F	T	E	F	F
f	f	l	f	k

Directions: In each row, circle the letters that are the same as the first letter in the row.

Visual discrimination of capital and lowercase e and f   19

Matching Letters

Name _____

E e elephant   F f fish

E	e	n	e	o
e	M	E	H	E
F	f	h	l	f
f	A	F	T	F

Directions: Look at the letter at the beginning of each row. Circle the letters in that row that belong with the first letter.

20   Matching capital with lowercase e and f

Short *E*

Name _____

elephant

Eskimo	bat	sock	elbow
hat	elephant	bow	gate
egg	cup	duck	pumpkin

Directions: Name the pictures. Circle each picture whose name begins with the sound you hear at the beginning of *elephant*.

Auditory discrimination of initial short e   21

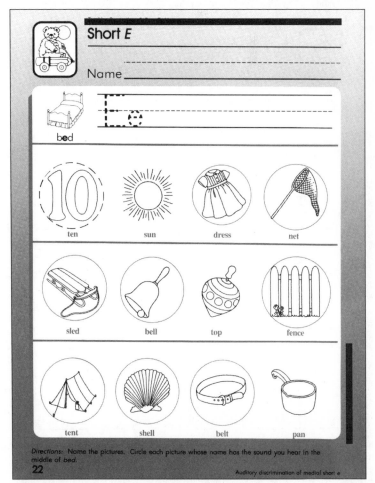

Short *E*

Name _____

bed

ten	sun	dress	net
sled	bell	top	fence
tent	shell	belt	pan

Directions: Name the pictures. Circle each picture whose name has the sound you hear in the middle of *bed*.

22   Auditory discrimination of medial short e

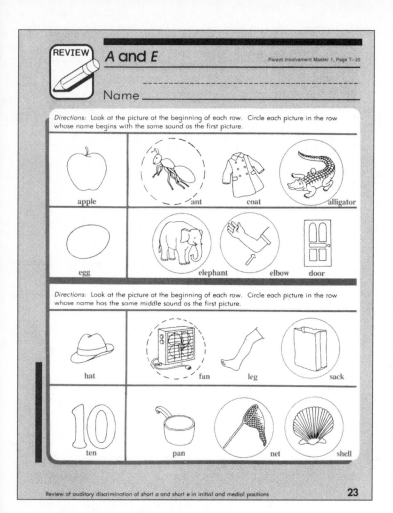

A and E

Parent Involvement Master 1, Page T–25

Name _____

Directions: Look at the picture at the beginning of each row. Circle each picture in the row whose name begins with the same sound as the first picture.

apple · ant · coat · alligator

egg · elephant · elbow · door

Directions: Look at the picture at the beginning of each row. Circle each picture in the row whose name has the same middle sound as the first picture.

hat · fan · leg · sack

ten · pan · net · shell

Review of auditory discrimination of short a and short e in initial and medial positions   **23**

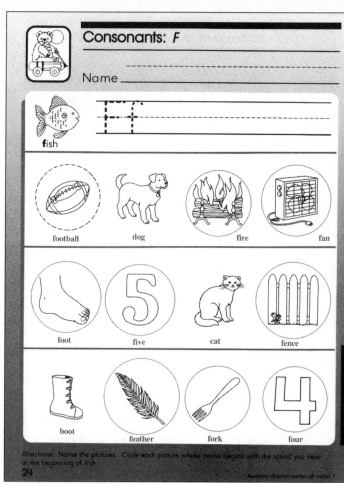

Consonants: F

Name _____

fish

football · dog · fire · fan

foot · five · cat · fence

boot · feather · fork · four

24   *Directions:* Name the pictures. Circle each picture whose name begins with the sound you hear at the beginning of *fish.*

Auditory discrimination of initial f

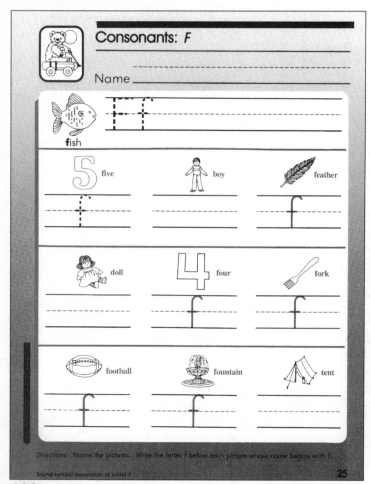

Consonants: F

Name _____

fish

five · boy · feather

doll · four · fork

football · fountain · tent

Directions: Name the pictures. Write the letter f below each picture whose name begins with f.

Sound-symbol association of initial f   **25**

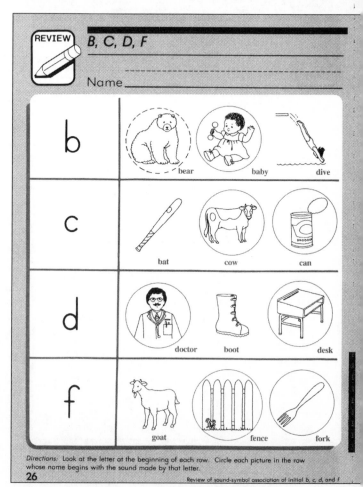

B, C, D, F

Name _____

b   bear · baby · dive

c   bat · cow · can

d   doctor · boot · desk

f   goat · fence · fork

26   *Directions:* Look at the letter at the beginning of each row. Circle each picture in the row whose name begins with the sound made by that letter.

Review of sound-symbol association of initial b, c, d, and f

Matching Letters

Name

G	C	G	F	G
g	g	y	g	j
H	H	L	I	H
h	d	h	h	l

Directions: In each row, circle the letters that are the same as the first letter in the row.
Visual discrimination of capital and lowercase g and h   27

Matching Letters

Name

G	g	d	g	y
g	Q	G	S	G
H	k	l	h	h
h	H	A	X	H

28   Directions: Look at the letter at the beginning of each row. Circle the letters in that row that belong with the first letter.
                                                   Matching capital with lowercase g and h

Consonants: G

Name

goat

goose   ladder   garage   gas pump

desk   garden   hammer   girl

game   five   gate   guitar

Directions: Name the pictures. Circle each picture whose name begins with the sound you hear at the beginning of goat.
Auditory discrimination of initial g   29

Consonants: G

Name

goat

game   goose   hat

gas pump   cow   garden

book   girl   garage

30   Directions: Name the pictures. Write the letter g below each picture whose name begins with g.
                                                   Sound-symbol association of initial g

Consonants: *H*

Name

horse

ham	hat	lock	house
hammer	kite	horn	hand
guitar	hose	helicopter	hanger

Directions: Name the pictures. Circle each picture whose name begins with the sound you hear at the beginning of *horse*.

Auditory discrimination of initial *h*

31

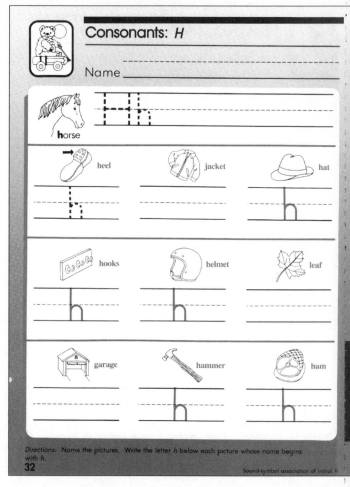

Consonants: *H*

Name

horse

heel	jacket	hat
hooks	helmet	leaf
garage	hammer	ham

Directions: Name the pictures. Write the letter *h* below each picture whose name begins with *h*.

32

Sound-symbol association of initial *h*

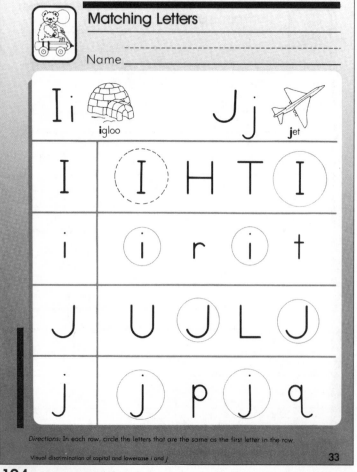

Matching Letters

Name

I i **i**gloo **J j** **j**et

I	I H T I
i	i r i t
J	U J L J
j	j p j q

Directions: In each row, circle the letters that are the same as the first letter in the row.

Visual discrimination of capital and lowercase *i* and *j*

33

Matching Letters

Name

I i **i**gloo **J j** **j**et

I	t i r
i	I V H I
J	i j p j
j	U J J L

Directions: Look at the letter at the beginning of each row. Circle the letters in that row that belong with the first letter.

34

Matching capital with lowercase *i* and *j*

104

Short I

Name _____

igloo

ink	candle	fan	ax
lamp	elephant	insects	ball
key	igloo	umbrella	hat

Directions: Name the pictures. Circle each picture whose name begins with the sound you hear at the beginning of *igloo.*

Auditory discrimination of initial short *i*

35

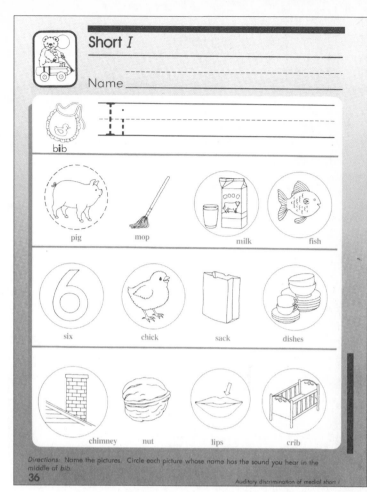

Short I

Name _____

bib

pig	mop	milk	fish
six	chick	sack	dishes
chimney	nut	lips	crib

Directions: Name the pictures. Circle each picture whose name has the sound you hear in the middle of *bib.*

36

Auditory discrimination of medial short *i*

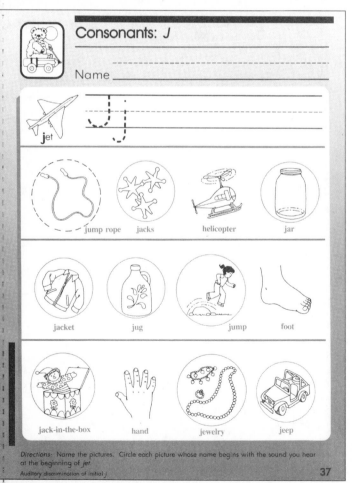

Consonants: *J*

Name _____

jet

jump rope	jacks	helicopter	jar
jacket	jug	jump	foot
jack-in-the-box	hand	jewelry	jeep

Directions: Name the pictures. Circle each picture whose name begins with the sound you hear at the beginning of *jet.*

Auditory discrimination of initial *j*

37

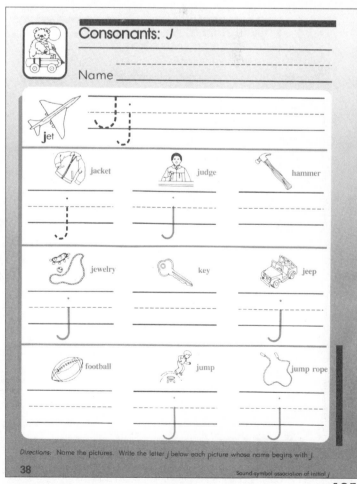

Consonants: *J*

Name _____

jet

jacket	judge	hammer
jewelry	key	jeep
football	jump	jump rope

Directions: Name the pictures. Write the letter *j* below each picture whose name begins with *j.*

38

Sound-symbol association of initial *j*

Name _____

K	K N R K
k	k l k t
L	J L I L
l	b l l d

Directions: In each row, circle the letters that are the same as the first letter in the row.

Visual discrimination of capital and lowercase *k* and *l*   **39**

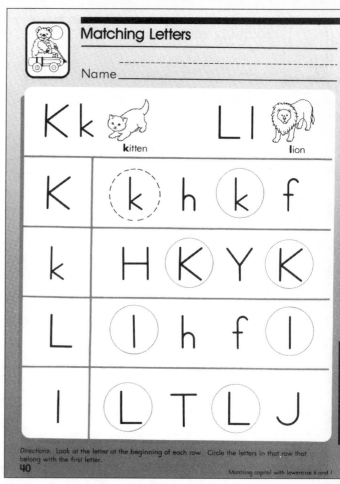

K	k h k f
k	H K Y K
L	l h f l
l	L T L J

40   *Directions:* Look at the letter at the beginning of each row. Circle the letters in that row that belong with the first letter.

Matching capital with lowercase *k* and *l*

Consonants: *K*

Name _____

kitten

key   garage   kangaroo   horse

kiss   feather   kite   king

ladder   kitchen   jeep   kick

Directions: Name the pictures. Circle each picture whose name begins with the sound you hear at the beginning of *kitten.*
Auditory discrimination of initial *k*   **41**

Consonants: *K*

Name _____

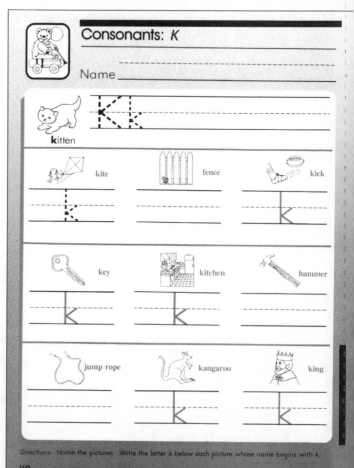

kitten

kite   fence   kick

key   kitchen   hammer

jump rope   kangaroo   king

Directions: Name the pictures. Write the letter *k* below each picture whose name begins with *k.*
42   Sound-symbol association of initial *k*

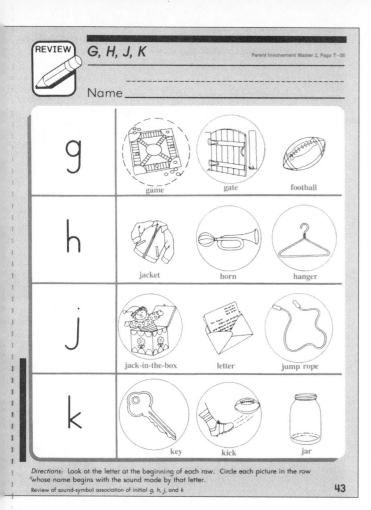

G, H, J, K

Parent Involvement Master 2, Page T-26

Name _____

g	game	gate	football
h	jacket	horn	hanger
j	jack-in-the-box	letter	jump rope
k	key	kick	jar

Directions: Look at the letter at the beginning of each row. Circle each picture in the row whose name begins with the sound made by that letter.

Review of sound-symbol association of initial *g, h, j,* and *k*

43

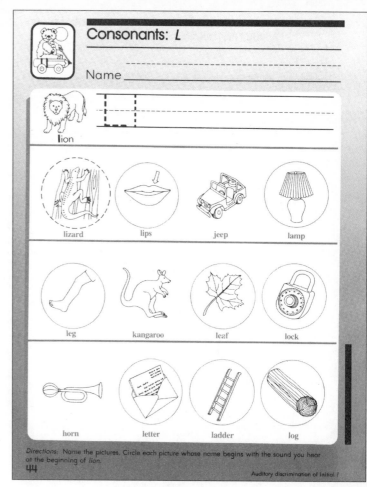

Consonants: *L*

Name _____

lion

lizard	lips	jeep	lamp
leg	kangaroo	leaf	lock
horn	letter	ladder	log

44

Directions: Name the pictures. Circle each picture whose name begins with the sound you hear at the beginning of *lion.*

Auditory discrimination of initial *l*

Consonants: *L*

Name _____

lion

lamp	dinosaur	log
jug	ladder	letter
leaf	lock	kite

Directions: Name the pictures. Write the letter *l* below each picture whose name begins with *l.*

Sound-symbol association of initial *l*

45

Matching Letters

Name _____

M m	mouse	N n	nest

M	W	M	H	M
m	m	h	w	m
N	V	N	N	M
n	n	m	u	n

46

Directions: In each row, circle the letters that are the same as the first letter in the row.

Visual discrimination of capital and lowercase *m* and *n*

107

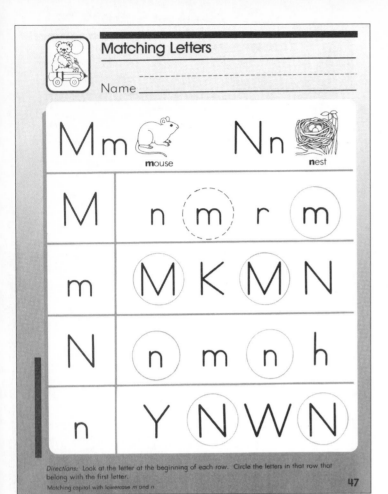

Matching Letters

Name _____

M	n (m) r (m)
m	(M) K (M) N
N	(n) m (n) h
n	Y (N) W (N)

Directions: Look at the letter at the beginning of each row. Circle the letters in that row that belong with the first letter.

Matching capital with lowercase *m* and *n*.

47

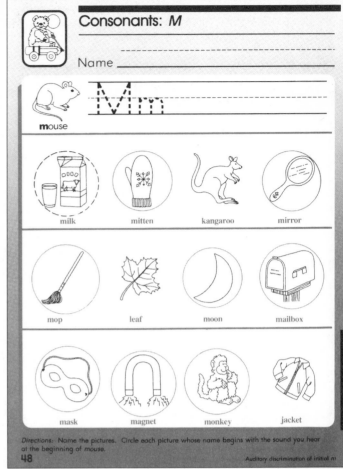

Consonants: M

Name _____

mouse

Mm

milk — mitten — kangaroo — mirror

mop — leaf — moon — mailbox

mask — magnet — monkey — jacket

Directions: Name the pictures. Circle each picture whose name begins with the sound you hear at the beginning of *mouse*.

48

Auditory discrimination of initial *m*.

Consonants: M

Name _____

mouse

Mm

moon — key — mask

m — — m

leg — map — money

— m — m

man — monkey — judge

m — m —

Directions: Name the pictures. Write the letter *m* below each picture whose name begins with *m*.

Sound-symbol association of initial *m*.

49

Consonants: N

Name _____

nest

Nn

numbers — nose — mop — needle

neck — nail — nine — letter

net — goat — nurse — newspaper

Directions: Name the pictures. Circle each picture whose name begins with the sound you hear at the beginning of *nest*.

50

Auditory discrimination of initial *n*.

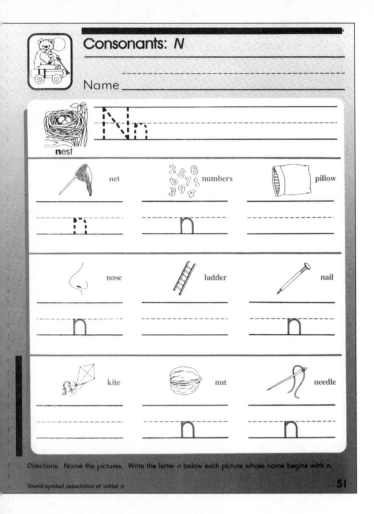

Consonants: N

Name

nest

net | **2 5 8 6 3 7 1 9 4** numbers | pillow

n | n |

nose | ladder | nail

n | | n

kite | nut | needle

| n | n

Directions: Name the pictures. Write the letter *n* below each picture whose name begins with *n*.

Sound-symbol association of initial *n*   **51**

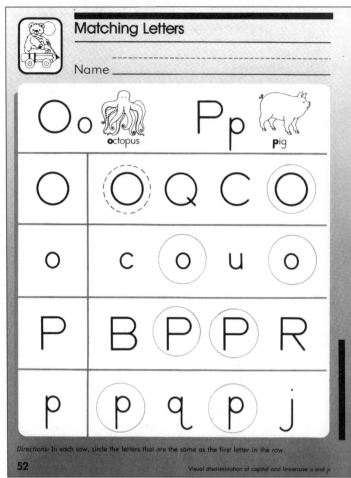

Matching Letters

Name

O o   **o**ctopus   P p   **p**ig

O | (O)   Q   C   (O)

o | c   (o)   u   (o)

P | B   (P)   (P)   R

p | (p)   q   (p)   j

Directions: In each row, circle the letters that are the same as the first letter in the row.

52   Visual discrimination of capital and lowercase *o* and *p*

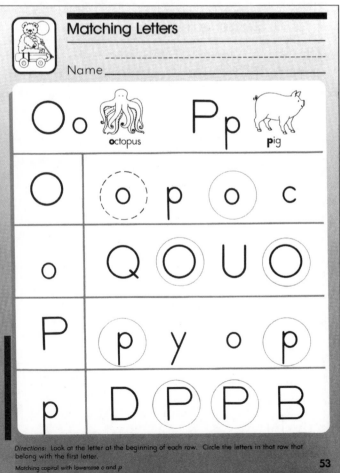

Matching Letters

Name

O o   **o**ctopus   P p   **p**ig

O | (o)   p   o   c

o | Q   (O)   U   (O)

P | (p)   y   o   (p)

p | D   (P)   (P)   B

Directions: Look at the letter at the beginning of each row. Circle the letters in that row that belong with the first letter.

Matching capital with lowercase *o* and *p*   **53**

Short O

Name

octopus

(ostrich) | hammer | lamp | pig

five | kite | (ox) | jug

gate | (octopus) | nail | mask

Directions: Name the pictures. Circle each picture whose name begins with the sound you hear at the beginning of *octopus*.

54   Auditory discrimination of initial short *o*

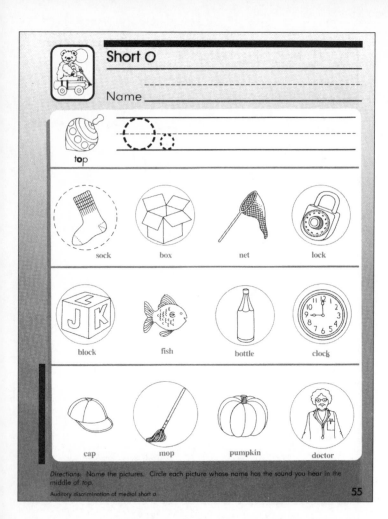

Short O

Name _____

top

sock	box	net	lock
block	fish	bottle	clock
cap	mop	pumpkin	doctor

Directions: Name the pictures. Circle each picture whose name has the sound you hear in the middle of *top*.

Auditory discrimination of medial short *o*.

55

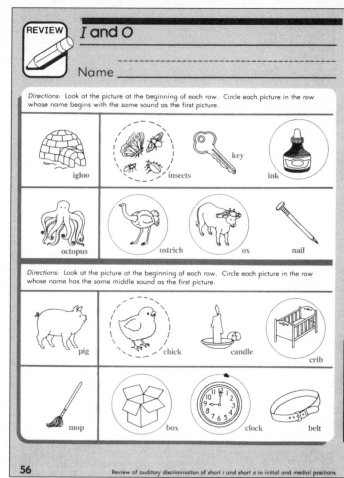

I and O

Name _____

Directions: Look at the picture at the beginning of each row. Circle each picture in the row whose name begins with the same sound as the first picture.

igloo	insects	key	ink
octopus	ostrich	ox	nail

Directions: Look at the picture at the beginning of each row. Circle each picture in the row whose name has the same middle sound as the first picture.

pig	chick	candle	crib
mop	box	clock	belt

56

Review of auditory discrimination of short *i* and short *o* in initial and medial positions

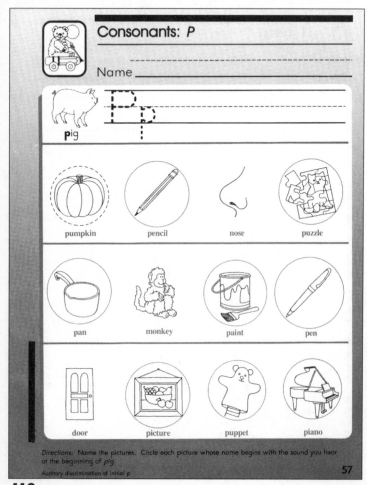

Consonants: P

Name _____

pig

pumpkin	pencil	nose	puzzle
pan	monkey	paint	pen
door	picture	puppet	piano

Directions: Name the pictures. Circle each picture whose name begins with the sound you hear at the beginning of *pig*.

Auditory discrimination of initial *p*

57

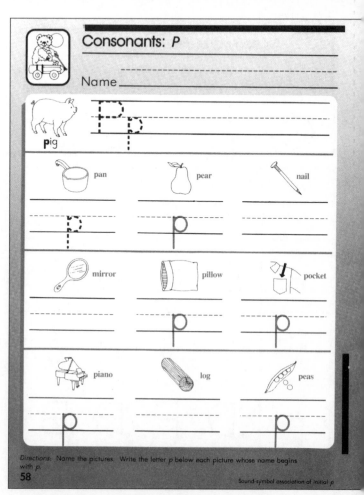

Consonants: P

Name _____

pig

pan	pear	nail
mirror	pillow	pocket
piano	log	peas

Directions: Name the pictures. Write the letter *p* below each picture whose name begins with *p*.

58

Sound-symbol association of initial *p*

110

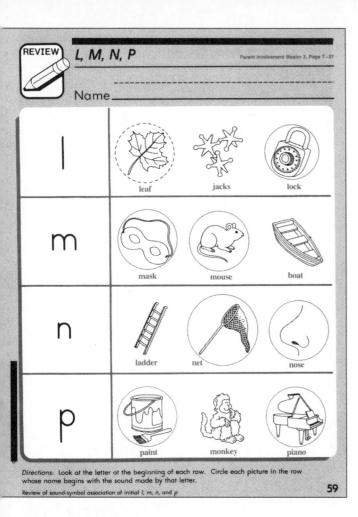

L, M, N, P

Parent Involvement Master 3, Page T-27

Name

Directions: Look at the letter at the beginning of each row. Circle each picture in the row whose name begins with the sound made by that letter.

Review of sound-symbol association of initial l, m, n, and p

59

Matching Letters

Name

Directions: In each row, circle the letters that are the same as the first letter in the row.

60

Visual discrimination of capital and lowercase q and r

Matching Letters

Name

Directions: Look at the letter at the beginning of each row. Circle the letters in that row that belong with the first letter.

Matching capital with lowercase q and r

61

Consonants: Qu

Name

Directions: Name the pictures. Circle each picture whose name begins with the sound you hear at the beginning of quilt.

62

Auditory discrimination of initial qu

111

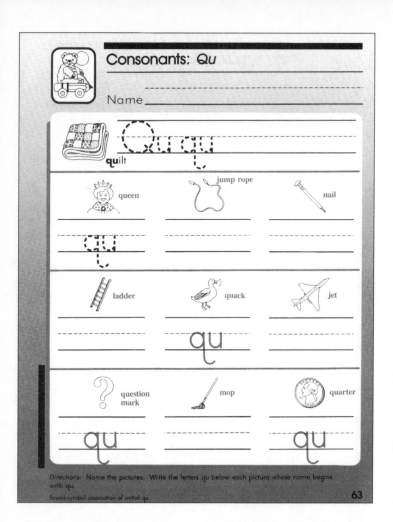

Consonants: Qu

Name _____

quilt

queen

jump rope

nail

ladder

quack

jet

qu

question mark

mop

quarter

qu

qu

Directions: Name the pictures. Write the letters *qu* below each picture whose name begins with *qu*.

Sound-symbol association of initial *qu*

63

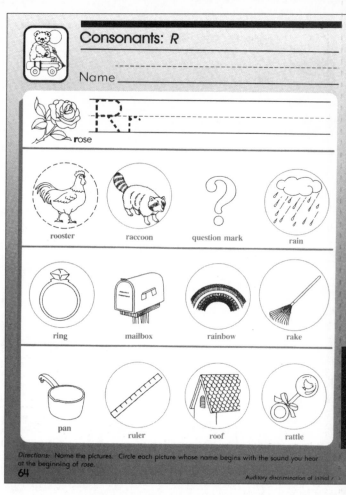

Consonants: R

Name _____

rose

rooster

raccoon

question mark

rain

ring

mailbox

rainbow

rake

pan

ruler

roof

rattle

Directions: Name the pictures. Circle each picture whose name begins with the sound you hear at the beginning of *rose*.

64

Auditory discrimination of initial *r*

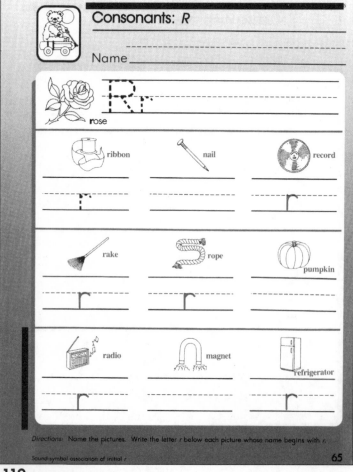

Consonants: R

Name _____

rose

ribbon

nail

record

r

r

rake

rope

pumpkin

r

r

radio

magnet

refrigerator

r

r

Directions: Name the pictures. Write the letter *r* below each picture whose name begins with *r*.

Sound-symbol association of initial *r*

65

Matching Letters

Name _____

S s		T t	
sun		**t**ent	
S	S	Z	G	S
s	z	s	e	s
T	T	L	T	Y
t	h	t	t	l

Directions: In each row, circle the letters that are the same as the first letter in the row.

66

Visual discrimination of capital and lowercase *s* and *t*

Matching Letters

Name _____

Ss	☼ sun	Tt	⛺ tent
S	(s) c (s) o
s	G (S) C (S)
T	I (t) (t) i
t	(T) Y (T) X

Directions: Look at the letter at the beginning of each row. Circle the letters in that row that belong with the first letter.

Matching capital with lowercase *s* and *t*

67

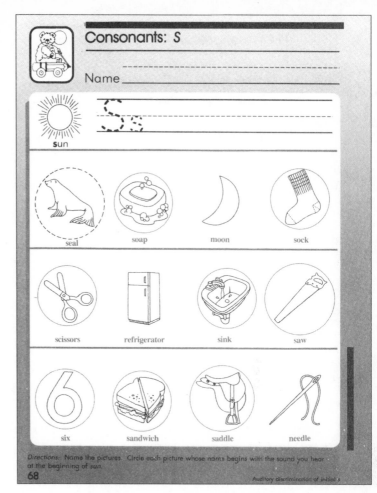

Consonants: S

Name _____

☼ sun Ss

seal	soap	moon	sock
scissors	refrigerator	sink	saw
six	sandwich	saddle	needle

68

Directions: Name the pictures. Circle each picture whose name begins with the sound you hear at the beginning of *sun.*

Auditory discrimination of initial *s*

Consonants: S

Name _____

☼ sun Ss

sink _____	mitten _____	sand _____
_____	_____	S
seven _____	saw _____	puppet _____
S	S	_____
rake _____	scissors _____	soap _____
_____	S	S

Directions: Name the pictures. Write the letter *s* below each picture whose name begins with *s.*

Sound-symbol association of initial *s*

69

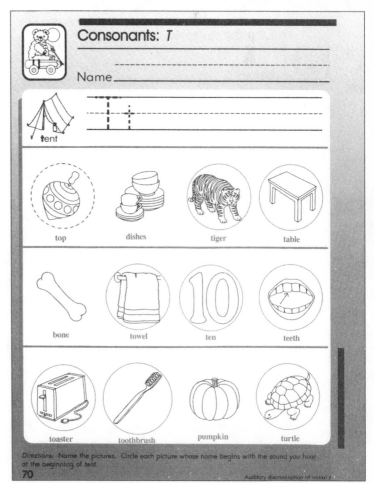

Consonants: T

Name _____

⛺ tent Tt

top	dishes	tiger	table
bone	towel	ten	teeth
toaster	toothbrush	pumpkin	turtle

70

Directions: Name the pictures. Circle each picture whose name begins with the sound you hear at the beginning of *tent.*

Auditory discrimination of initial *t*

113

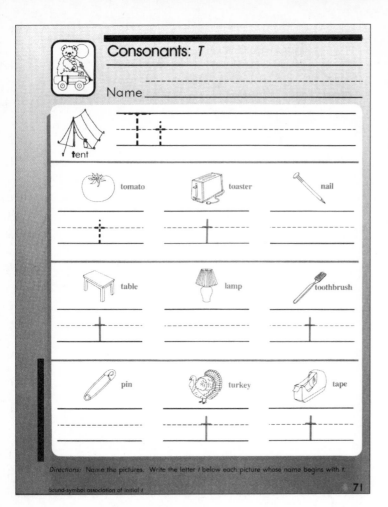

Consonants: T

Name

tent

tomato	toaster	nail
lamp	table	toothbrush
pin	turkey	tape

Directions: Name the pictures. Write the letter *t* below each picture whose name begins with *t*.

Sound-symbol association of initial *t*

71

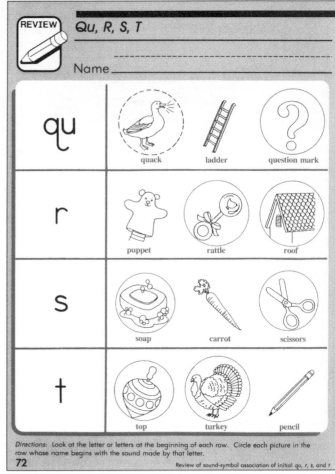

Qu, R, S, T

Name

qu	quack	ladder	question mark
r	puppet	rattle	roof
s	soap	carrot	scissors
t	top	turkey	pencil

Directions: Look at the letter or letters at the beginning of each row. Circle each picture in the row whose name begins with the sound made by that letter.

72   Review of sound-symbol association of initial *qu, r, s,* and *t*

Matching Letters

Name

U u umbrella   V v vase

U	O	U	J	U
u	u	n	c	u
V	X	V	V	N
v	v	u	z	v

Directions: In each row, circle the letters that are the same as the first letter in the row.

Visual discrimination of capital and lowercase *u* and *v*

73

Matching Letters

Name

U u umbrella   V v vase

U	v	u	n	u
u	U	O	U	C
V	w	v	u	v
v	V	N	Y	V

Directions: Look at the letter at the beginning of each row. Circle the letters in that row that belong with the first letter.

74   Matching capital with lowercase *u* and *v*

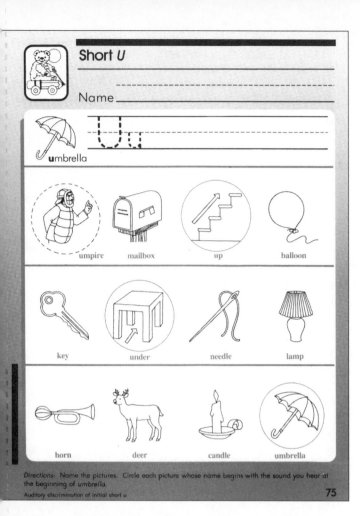

Short *U*

Name _____

umbrella

umpire	mailbox	up	balloon
key	under	needle	lamp
horn	deer	candle	umbrella

Directions: Name the pictures. Circle each picture whose name begins with the sound you hear at the beginning of *umbrella*.

Auditory discrimination of initial short *u*

75

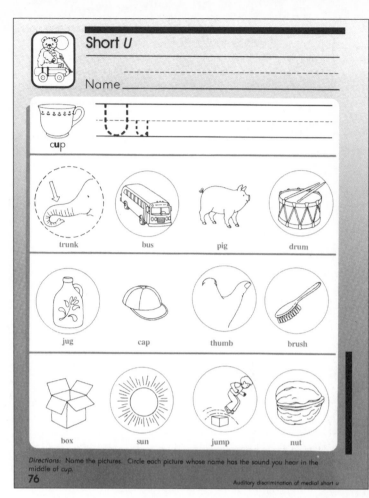

Short *U*

Name _____

c**u**p

trunk	bus	pig	drum
jug	cap	thumb	brush
box	sun	jump	nut

Directions: Name the pictures. Circle each picture whose name has the sound you hear in the middle of *cup*.

76

Auditory discrimination of medial short *u*

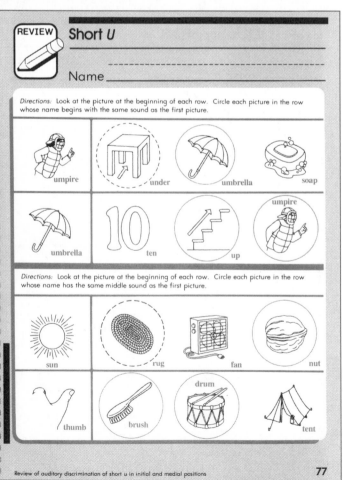

REVIEW Short *U*

Name _____

Directions: Look at the picture at the beginning of each row. Circle each picture in the row whose name begins with the same sound as the first picture.

umpire	under	umbrella	soap
umbrella	ten	up	umpire

Directions: Look at the picture at the beginning of each row. Circle each picture in the row whose name has the same middle sound as the first picture.

sun	rug	fan	nut
thumb	brush	drum	tent

Review of auditory discrimination of short *u* in initial and medial positions

77

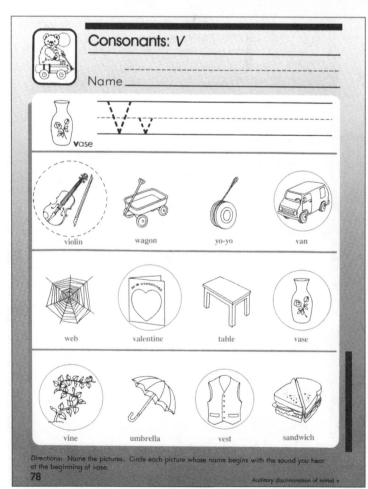

Consonants: *V*

Name _____

vase

violin	wagon	yo-yo	van
web	valentine	table	vase
vine	umbrella	vest	sandwich

Directions: Name the pictures. Circle each picture whose name begins with the sound you hear at the beginning of *vase*.

78

Auditory discrimination of initial *v*

Consonants: V

Name _____

vase

vest	vine	raccoon
violin	turtle	valentine
saddle	vase	van

Directions: Name the pictures. Write the letter v below each picture whose name begins with v.

Sound-symbol association of initial v

79

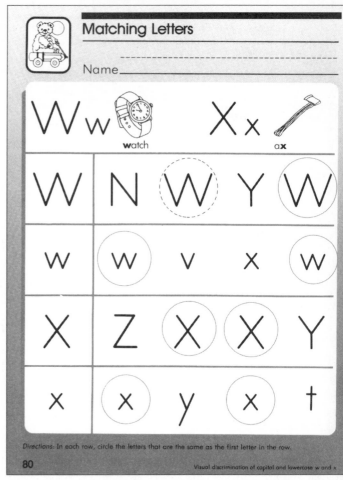

Matching Letters

Name _____

Ww watch   Xx ax

W	N	⟨W⟩	Y	⟨W⟩
w	⟨w⟩	v	x	⟨w⟩
X	Z	⟨X⟩	⟨X⟩	Y
x	⟨x⟩	y	⟨x⟩	†

Directions: In each row, circle the letters that are the same as the first letter in the row.

80   Visual discrimination of capital and lowercase w and x

Matching Letters

Name _____

Ww watch   Xx ax

W	v	⟨w⟩	m	⟨w⟩
w	⟨W⟩	K	⟨W⟩	Z
X	⟨x⟩	†	v	⟨x⟩
x	Y	⟨X⟩	Z	⟨X⟩

Directions: Look at the letter at the beginning of each row. Circle the letters in that row that belong with the first letter.

Matching capital with lowercase w and x   81

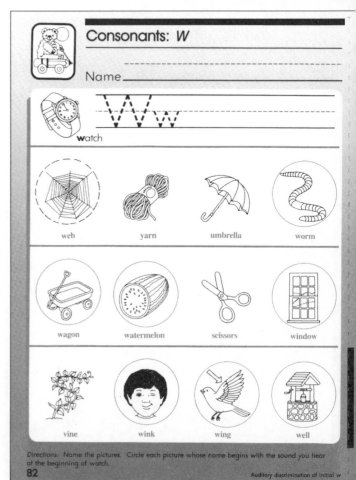

Consonants: W

Name _____

watch

web	yarn	umbrella	worm
wagon	watermelon	scissors	window
vine	wink	wing	well

Directions: Name the pictures. Circle each picture whose name begins with the sound you hear at the beginning of watch.

82   Auditory discrimination of initial w

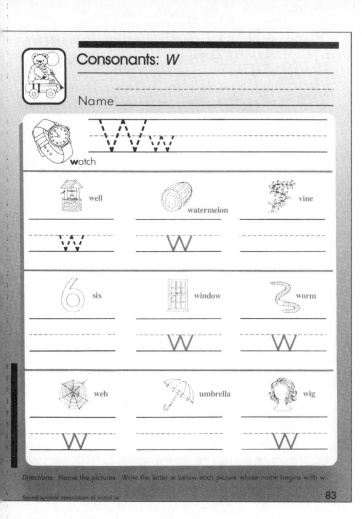

Consonants: W

Name _____

watch

well	watermelon	vine
W	W	
six	window	worm
	W	W
web	umbrella	wig
W		W

Directions: Name the pictures. Write the letter w below each picture whose name begins with w.

Sound-symbol association of initial w

83

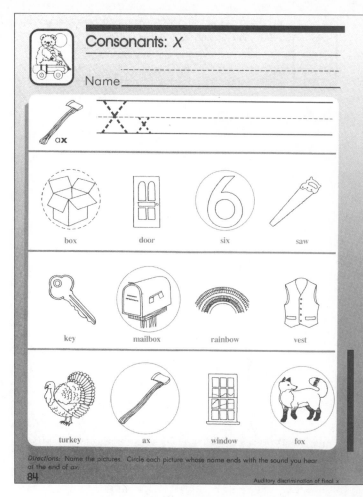

Consonants: X

Name _____

ax

box	door	six	saw
key	mailbox	rainbow	vest
turkey	ax	window	fox

Directions: Name the pictures. Circle each picture whose name ends with the sound you hear at the end of ax.

84

Auditory discrimination of final x

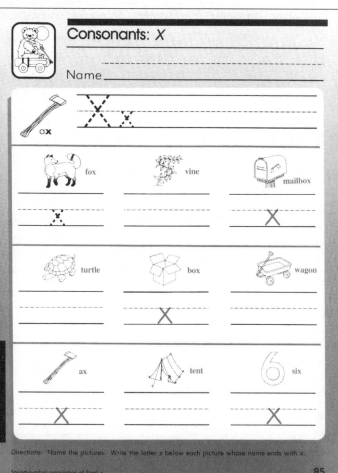

Consonants: X

Name _____

ax

fox	vine	mailbox
X		X
turtle	box	wagon
	X	
ax	tent	six
X		X

Directions: Name the pictures. Write the letter x below each picture whose name ends with x.

Sound-symbol association of final x

85

Matching Letters

Name _____

Yy   yard   Zz   zoo

Y	Y	T	K	Y
y	v	y	w	y
Z	Z	N	Z	I
z	Z	S	W	Z

Directions: In each row, circle the letters that are the same as the first letter in the row.

86

Visual discrimination of capital and lowercase y and z

117

Matching Letters

Name

Y	x	(y)	h	(y)
y	(Y)	T	(Y)	K
Z	s	(z)	(z)	c
z	N	(Z)	I	(Z)

Directions: Look at the letter at the beginning of each row. Circle the letters in that row that belong with the first letter.

Matching capital with lowercase y and z

87

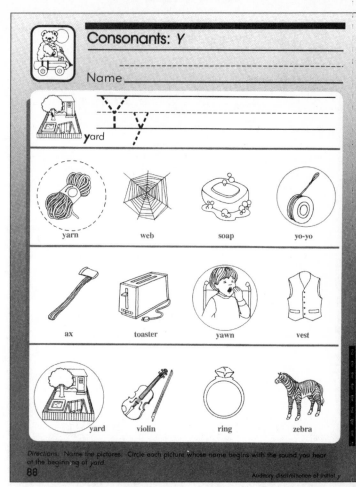

Consonants: Y

Name

yard

yarn	web	soap	yo-yo
ax	toaster	yawn	vest
yard	violin	ring	zebra

Directions: Name the pictures. Circle each picture whose name begins with the sound you hear at the beginning of yard.

88

Auditory discrimination of initial y

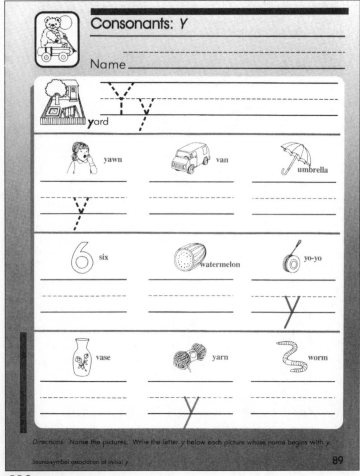

Consonants: Y

Name

yard

yawn	van	umbrella
six	watermelon	yo-yo
vase	yarn	worm

Directions: Name the pictures. Write the letter y below each picture whose name begins with y.

Sound-symbol association of initial y

89

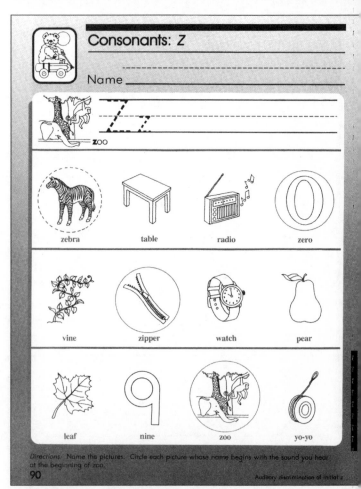

Consonants: Z

Name

zoo

zebra	table	radio	zero
vine	zipper	watch	pear
leaf	nine	zoo	yo-yo

Directions: Name the pictures. Circle each picture whose name begins with the sound you hear at the beginning of zoo.

90

Auditory discrimination of initial z

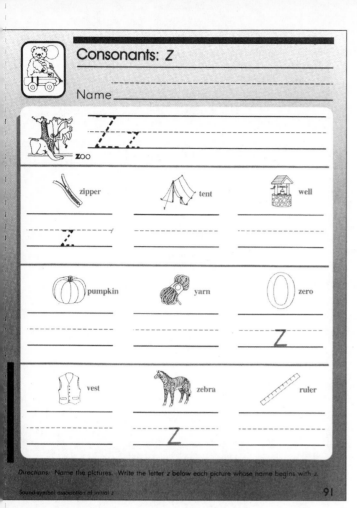

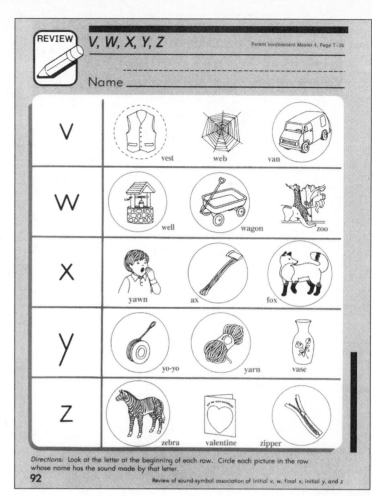

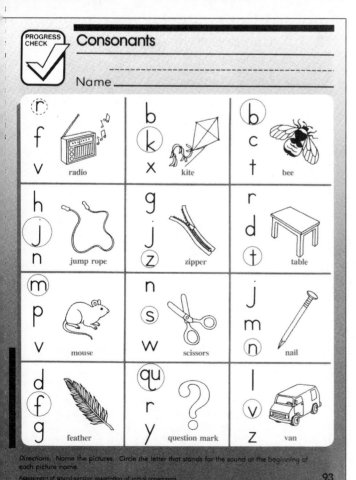

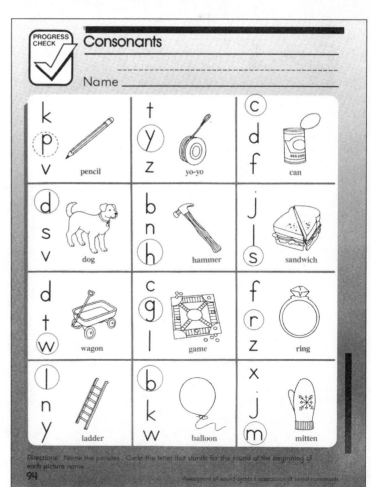

119

Vowels

Name _____

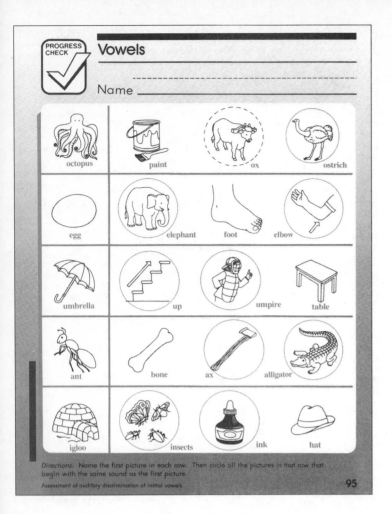

Directions: Name the first picture in each row. Then circle all the pictures in that row that begin with the same sound as the first picture.

Assessment of auditory discrimination of initial vowels

95

120

NOTES

NOTES

NOTES

NOTES

NOTES

NOTES